ex libris

Little Lost Nun

Melinda Johnson

PARK END BOOKS

2021

Cover & interior illustrations: David Moses
Cover & interior illustrations copyright ©2021 David Moses

Publisher's Cataloging-in-Publication Data
Names: Johnson, Melinda, 1972-, Author
Title: Little Lost Nun
Description: Sugar Land [Texas]: Park End Books, 2021.

Identifiers: ISBN: 978-1-953427-17-5

Subjects: JUVENILE FICTION/Religious/Christian/Friendship

www.ParkEndBooks.com

For Jennifer Irene, with so much love.

The Lord will give strength unto His people. The Lord will bless His people with peace.

glossary

Gerontissa: This is a Greek word. A *gerontissa* is a wise elder. Often, she lives in and leads a monastery, a place where nuns live. She stays close to God in her heart, and the Holy Spirit can help her understand and speak to people.

Nun: A nun is a woman who gives her whole life to her church. She lives in a monastery with other nuns. She prays and sings and works every day. That is her job and her chosen place in the world.

Monastery: A monastery is a place where people live when they give their whole life to the church. Some monasteries are for nuns (women), and some are for monks (men). The monastery has its own church building and a building where the nuns live. Monasteries often have beautiful gardens.

Icon: An icon is a special kind of painting that tries to show people the way that God sees them when they have been transformed in His love. They are special because they show Jesus—who is God and human—the icon of the invisible God. A person who makes icons is called an iconographer. Icons show pictures of holy people, stories from the Bible, miracles, and other events in Christian history. If you visit an Orthodox church, you will see icons hanging on the walls, painted on the ceiling, and standing in a row near the altar.

Morning prayers: This is the first service of the day in an Orthodox church or monastery. A monastery church holds services every day, several times a day. Everyone comes together to pray these prayers.

Refectory: This is the dining room at the monastery where the nuns eat their meals.

Dormition: Dormition is a word that means "going to sleep." In the Orthodox church, when someone you love dies, you say that person fell asleep in the Lord. A person who is asleep in the Lord will wake up again in heaven. On August 15, the Orthodox church remembers the day Mary, the Mother of God, fell asleep in the Lord and woke up in heaven.

Feast: In the Orthodox church, a feast is a holy day when we remember something special. Christmas is a feast, Easter is a feast, and in this story, the nuns celebrate the Dormition feast, which celebrates Mary going to heaven. There is a church service for each feast, and there also are traditions people follow in honor of the day.

Almsgiver: Alms are money or gifts given to someone who needs them. An almsgiver is a person who gives alms to people in need.

Saints: Saints are holy people, on earth or in heaven. To be holy means to become like God by being near God. A saint is a person who loves God and chooses to be near Him. God's love shines in the saint's heart and on everyone around that person.

Holy Family: This is a name for the family Jesus had when He was born on earth, including His mother Mary, Joseph who was married to Mary and took care of Jesus as His father and protector on earth, Joseph's children who became Jesus' brothers and sisters, and Jesus. Jesus lived as the child of Mary and Joseph, and some icons show Mary, Joseph, and Joseph's son James along with Jesus.

Mother of God: This is a respectful and loving name for Mary, the woman who gave birth to Jesus and took care of Him as He grew up, because Jesus is God as well as human.

St. Nicholas: St. Nicholas was a Christian bishop who lived in the 3rd and 4th century. People all over the world love St. Nicholas because he cares about people and performs miracles for them. The modern "Santa Claus" is based on stories from St. Nicholas' life.

St. Tabitha and St. Peter: The little nun in this story is holding an icon showing a story from the Bible. The story is in the Book of Acts (chapter 9, verses 36-41). Tabitha was a woman who took care of the poor. She got sick and died, and her friends were sad. Peter was one of the 12 Apostles of Christ. He came to Tabitha, and brought her back to life.

chapter one

At the Monastery of Saint Tabitha the Almsgiver, the Gerontissa is very old. She rarely speaks, but her heart and her mind are clear. She loves to welcome visitors to the monastery, especially children, and sometimes, she surprises them by knowing things only the Holy Spirit could have told her.

There are three gardens at the monastery, a vegetable garden to feed the nuns and their guests, a prayer garden planted with fragrant herbs and flowers, and a children's garden that follows a wandering flagstone path through the trees and around the pond.

There is a blessing on the children's garden. A little breeze lives there, rustling the branches, scattering coins of sunlight along the path. The words of saints are painted on stones and carved on trees along the winding way. A miniature church with a tea-cup-sized dome rests on a miniature mountain beside the path. Tiny wooden nuns climb the mountain, carrying tiny icons. Nearby, a finger-sized Moses stands by a fist-sized boulder, holding up his staff to bring water from the rock. St. Nicholas walks the deck of a model ship, poised on the edge of the pond. The Holy Family, carefully carved and painted, travel toward a small cave made of smooth river stones.

The Gerontissa often comes to this garden with the children who visit the monastery. Sometimes, the monastery kittens follow them, darting and scampering along the path. But early each morning, the Gerontissa comes to the garden alone, to the miniature church with the teacup-sized dome.

She finds herself in the procession on the rock, a tiny Gerontissa leading the sisters to their prayers. Her gaze lingers on the nun that carries a tiny copy of the monastery's special icon of St. Tabitha, and the Gerontissa's heart shows her countless children joining the procession, following that little figure on her path to the church door.

The Gerontissa leans forward, her gnarled fingers blessing each little sister, from last to first. She crosses herself, closing her eyes, and her kind, wrinkled face is full of joy.

❦ ❦ ❦ ❦ ❦

For many years, the little nun stood in procession with her sisters, her tiny hands clasping the beautiful icon, her eyes fixed on the little church. In the beginning, there was no sign she would not be like the others.

On the day when the little nun left the procession, the birds sang cheerfully at dawn. The koi swam peacefully in the pond. Puffs of warm air caressed the children's garden and fluttered the petals of shade-loving flowers.

It was August 14th, the day before the Dormition Feast. Anticipation sparkled in the air. In morning prayers, in daily tasks, the monastery nuns kept their inward eyes on the Holy Mother of God.

At 10:00 am, a nun crossing the courtyard near the

front gate saw a procession of cars coming up the lane. Their wheels crunched on the gravel, and long grasses brushed them from the roadside.

Three cars pulled into the graveled lot in front of the gate. The nun smiled at the cars, hearing the stillness as the engines fell silent and the voices as the car doors opened. These were expected guests. She hastened to the Gerontissa.

When the Gerontissa reached the gate, she beamed and nodded in every direction. Each time a car door opened and a woman or child stepped out, the Gerontissa smiled at her and reached out her hands. Her prayers continued on the inside, so she did not use many words, but her guests felt the warmth of her welcome.

There were twelve women, tying scarves over their hair, shaking out wrinkled skirts, and gathering up their gifts of food for the nuns. Each had several children with her – all daughters. The sons and fathers were at home, letting this day before the Holy Mother's feast be a pilgrimage of women.

Most of the children knew the Gerontissa well, and she held out her hands to them as they buzzed around her like friendly bees, hoping, like bees, to reach their garden. Only two girls kept quiet in this happy swarm, and their mothers were quiet also, standing behind them.

The first girl wore a short blue dress, too small for her, and her legs seemed thin and bruised in the brief shadow cast around her by the wrinkled skirt. The second girl wore a clean white dress, and her mother tied a lace kerchief over her dark hair as she stood watching the other children. She peered out from under her mother's hands, then skipped away.

"You come with me," she told the first girl. "I can show you." She led the way down the path after the happy crowd, walking too fast for her smaller companion. The girl in the blue dress took hasty, running steps, making her shorter legs keep pace with her determined guide.

The Gerontissa, glancing back, saw the two mothers following their daughters. One woman frowned slightly, and the other tried to smile. They didn't speak, but they kept pace with each other in the milling group of women.

Reaching the prayer garden first, the Gerontissa turned to the mothers, gesturing to them like a hostess displaying a bountiful feast. *Here*, said her hands, *here is the prayer garden for you, and there,* said her hands again, *there is the children's garden where your girls will be safe and happy while you rest.* The mothers nodded and smiled and crossed themselves, and they drifted away from the path into the prayer garden. Only the two silent mothers hovered at the edge.

The children reached their garden, and their voices joined the threads of breeze and birdsong among the trees as they found each of the garden's treasures. Three girls sat down with St. Nicholas and his ship beside the pond. A tall, studious girl with a notebook and pencil skipped from tree to tree, laying the notebook pages on the engravings of saints' words and making rubbings of them with her pencil. The youngest children found the Holy Family and knelt on the moss to sing them chirping songs of love.

The bruised girl in the blue dress and her dutiful friend reached the garden after the other children.

"Did you know this place has the same name as you?" asked the girl in the white dress, making conversation.

The bruised girl shook her head.

"It does, you know," her friend persevered. "This is Tabitha's monastery, just like you're Tabitha."

"Tabby, mostly. Only you call me Tabitha."

"Well, I do it because it's your name."

Tabitha pulled at her short skirt and gazed at her shoes.

Her friend let her eyes wander into the garden, then over her shoulder to where she could see their mothers hovering beside the prayer garden. She let her face crinkle into a doubtful look, and her mother gestured at her. *Go into the garden, Nina,* said her mother's hands. *Be a good friend and take Tabby with you.*

Nina sighed. She patted Tabitha's shoulder. "Do

you want to see my favorite part?"

Tabitha reached out her hand, and Nina grasped it and started walking again, to the little holy mountain with its blue-domed church and its procession of wooden nuns.

Sunbeams filtering through green leaves above the girls dappled the church and the mountain with light. Nina and Tabitha gazed at the tiny nuns - dull black robes, silver crosses the size of a zipper's tooth, silver chains like darning thread, round faces with eyes painted black or brown, or painted shut with feathery lashes resting on the wooden cheeks of little nuns who prayed as they processed. Moss crept over the mountain, covering the painted rock.

Nina knelt in the grass and folded her hands. Her eyes traveled with loving care from one detail to the next. She breathed and closed her eyes. It was the best place in her world, and the most beloved.

The Gerontissa saw her kneeling by the church and smiled. She knew every child's favorite place in the garden, and perhaps she knew what made them choose these places. Her heart warmed to Nina, and she started

13

down the path to share her joy.

At that moment, something happened.

Tabitha reached over Nina's shoulder and snatched a nun out of the procession. With a snap, like a dry branch breaking under foot, the little nun sprang from her place on the rock and disappeared into Tabitha's closed fist. The little icon dropped soundlessly onto the mossy mountain.

Nina screamed.

Tabitha began to run.

The Gerontissa could not move quickly enough across the garden. Children, happily unaware, clutched her fingers and her robes. Nina lunged after Tabitha. They stumbled, one after the other, and scrambled up, racing down the path toward the graveled parking lot, forgetting their mothers standing by the prayer garden.

But the mothers snatched their daughters as they passed, stopping their headlong flight.

"She took a nun! She broke it!" panted Nina, smearing the tears across her cheeks with shaking fingers.

14

"Give it back, Tabitha! You ruined everything!"

Tabitha stared at the ground, and her mother grasped her arm and shook her. "What did you do? Answer me now! What did you do?"

"She took a nun! Look in her hand," cried Nina.

Tabitha's mother slapped her daughter's hands frantically, her face red and her shoulders hunched against the watching eyes of the women who were streaming out of the prayer garden.

Tabitha flinched, but she said nothing and she did not uncurl her hands. Tabitha's mother seized her shoulder and half dragged her away, down the path, scolding and shouting.

Everyone stood still.

The breeze rustled the leaves. Nina sobbed. A car door slammed. The engine started, and the gravel hissed under the flying wheels as Tabitha's mother drove away.

Nina threw herself into her mother's arms. "She took the nun! She didn't give it back!"

The mothers shook their heads, the children stared

solemnly at Nina, and the Gerontissa shepherded them all across the gravel lot to a small chapel on the other side. She tried to feed them, after their prayers, but they went away soon, sad and quiet.

The Little Nun Doll

chapter two

Tabitha leaned into the corner of the backseat as the car swung out of the parking lot.

"You're trouble! *Nothing* but trouble. I can't go *anywhere* with you," shouted her mother, banging her hands on the steering wheel. Tabitha gazed at the cracks in the vinyl seat back in front of her. There was no point in talking to grownups.

She felt the smooth hard shape of the little wooden nun inside her closed hand.

"I could find somewhere good to live if I didn't have a kid. Somebody at that church could take me in, but nobody wants you around when you have a kid." Her

18

mother leaned on the horn and stepped on the gas. The car roared past a startled couple walking their dog by the side of the road. "Stupid people. Can't they see this car coming? It's so big it needs oars! Are they blind?"

Tabitha kept her eyes on the seat back and slowly moved one hand to the hem of her dress. She tried to think casual, innocent thoughts. Sometimes, she worried that her thoughts would show on her face and draw attention to her. She flicked the hem over. It was about an inch wide, and the stitching was loose in several places. She glanced at her mother.

"What did you do, anyway? That prissy little girl was screaming like you kicked her butt. Did you hit her or what?" Her mother turned in the seat, still driving full speed.

"No, ma'am.

"No, you didn't hit her?"

"No, ma'am." Tabitha's eyes flicked to the windshield.

Her mother laughed. "You hate when I don't look,

19

you little scaredy cat. You hate it. But I have eyes in the back of my head, and don't you forget it."

Tabitha kept her face blank. But in the far corner of her mind, where she kept her private thoughts, she explained to herself that if her mother *really* had eyes in the back of her head, that little wooden nun wouldn't still be clutched in Tabitha's hand. It would be gone. Thrown out the car window, most likely.

Tabitha sat motionless and silent. After a few perilous seconds, her mother turned back to her driving. Her anger burned fiercely, but never lasted long.

Nothing lasted, with Tabitha's mother. She couldn't keep her mind on anything. Tabitha remembered the day she had figured that out. It wasn't long ago, maybe a week after her eighth birthday. She'd been in trouble all day – too loud, too quiet, too ugly, too pretty, never where she was wanted, always where she wasn't wanted. In the middle of the afternoon, something clicked inside her mind. *Wait for a few minutes*, whispered the new thought. *She only pays attention for a few minutes at a time. She'll forget.*

And it was true. Tabitha watched the clock. Five minutes later, her mother had gone outside to smoke, and Tabitha was mercifully forgotten.

Now, she counted to sixty in her mind, giving her mother time to look out at the world beyond the windshield and fasten on something out there to distract and infuriate her.

"Look at those houses! Who needs a house that big? These people are filthy, filthy rich. They could fit the whole town in that house. I should go knock on the door..."

Tabitha moved her hand swiftly across her skirt and slipped the little wooden nun under the loose stitching, into the hem. She waited a few seconds, then poked her finger into the hole and pushed the little nun as far as she could, into a tighter spot where the thread looked stronger. Then she laid the hem across her knees again, making it look natural, and moved her hands away from it. The dress looked rumpled anyway. No one would notice.

When the car pulled into the trailer park where her grandfather lived, Tabitha had to close her eyes. The road was narrow, the trailers and their occupants crowded up along it on both sides. With her mother at the wheel, the car seemed huge and wild, like an animal careering through the jungle, likely to crush anything in its path.

"Look at this place. One double-wide after another." Her mother laughed. "Grandpa Pete didn't do very well for himself, did he?"

He did better than we did, thought Tabitha, *or we wouldn't be staying with him because we have no place else to go.*

The car finally stopped moving, but Tabitha waited until she heard the keys pull out of the ignition. Her mother sometimes turned the car on again just as Tabitha was opening the door to get out.

"Come on, slow poke."

In one swift motion, Tabitha threw open her door and jumped out. Then she turned and closed the door carefully.

"Harder! You know it won't latch unless you slam."

Gritting her teeth, Tabitha re-opened her door and

slammed it shut.

"Knock on the door. You know he won't give me a key."

Tabitha rapped on the screen door frame. Her mother reached over her shoulder and pulled the screen door open, almost knocking Tabitha over.

"Harder! He can't hear that."

Tabitha turned her fist to protect her knuckles and pounded the locked door with the side of her closed hand.

The door opened from the inside, but Grandpa Pete didn't say anything. He just left the door open and went back to his recliner in the corner of the front room. Tabitha's mother pushed past her into the house, and Tabitha came through the door quickly behind her. Her mother had shut her out once, as a joke.

Her mother turned suddenly. "You can take that dress off. No church people around here to impress, and you'll just mess it up if you keep on wearing it. Here, give it to me."

Tabitha froze.

"Come on. Just take it off now, and I'll put it with the laundry."

Tabitha's mind fumbled with words, looking for some that might work. She had to get the nun out of the hem of her dress without her mother knowing it was ever there.

Her mother took a step toward her. Unexpectedly, her grandfather spoke. "Not here. You go change in the bathroom, Tabby. Your mother's got manners like a badly trained dog."

In the second it took for her mother to spin around and start screaming an answer to this insult, Tabby raced out of the room, down the tiny hall to the bathroom. She locked herself into it and sank down on the floor.

Getting the nun back out was harder than she expected. Her fingers were shaky and sweaty, and the nun was wedged so tightly that Tabby had to squeeze her slowly down the hemline until she had worked the little wooden doll back to the place where the stitches had come loose. Her hands felt slower and slower. Any second, her mother might pound on the door, wanting to know what took so long.

With the nun finally loose in her hand, Tabby's eyes roamed over the bathroom. Where could she hide the nun? Nowhere in this room. She set the little doll on the floor beside her, then picked her up again and shoved her down into her sock, scraping her ankle. Tabby winced. She ripped off the dress and picked up the shorts and shirt she had taken off that morning, which were piled on the floor under the sink. The shorts had pockets. They were an old pair of jeans with the legs cut off. All of Tabby's clothes had to be worn long after they should have been discarded.

Gasping with relief, Tabby pulled on the shorts and stuffed the little nun into the pocket. She didn't tuck her shirt in. She let it hang out over the pockets. Then she grabbed the dress she had just taken off, took a deep breath, and opened the bathroom door.

Her mother was standing outside the door. She snatched the dress from Tabby's hands. "Give it here, Miss Priss. It's an old rag anyhow. Now get outside and let me have some peace."

Tabby ducked past her and ran for the door.

chapter three

Nina went straight to the window seat when she got home. It was her favorite place in the house, a cushioned alcove in the big bay window that faced the back yard. With the ease of long practice, she reached around the corner of the window alcove and pulled the cord to close the drapes, shutting herself in. She pushed aside two books she had been reading earlier in the day and wrapped her arms around her favorite cushion, an old red velvet one, lopsided with age. With a sigh of relief, she leaned her hot forehead against the smooth glass and shut her eyes.

There was a scuffling sound behind her, and Lucas, her six-year-old brother, poked himself between the drapes. "I saw you go in here. I'm coming in, too."

"Lucas, go away. Can't you see I want to be by myself?"

"So? You don't own the whole world."

"I don't want the whole world. I just want the window seat to myself."

Lucas clambered up beside her. "That's OK. I can read to you. I can read *Yertle the Turtle*."

Nina buried her face in her cushion. "Why?" she moaned. "Why is this day so BAD?"

"What happened? Why is it bad?"

Nina sighed and sat up, prepared to make an effort.

"It doesn't matter, Lucas. You weren't there."

"But now I'm here."

Nina stared out the window. Beyond the glass, she saw her father working in the garden. A tear slipped down her cheek. "I just had a bad day, that's all."

Lucas looked surprised. "But you were at the monastery."

"I know."

"How could you have a bad day at the monastery?

You always want to go there."

"I know."

"So? Did you fall down?"

"No, I didn't fall down. Just, something sad happened when I was there."

"What?" Lucas scooched himself further into the window seat, until his back was against the glass. "Tell."

Nina sniffed. "You know that garden where we go?"

"The one with Moses and the rock?"

"Yes, and St. Nicholas and his boat at the fish pond. That one. Well, you know how my favorite part is the church with the little nuns?"

Lucas nodded. He knew.

"This girl who came with us broke it!"

Lucas started. "She *broke* it? How could she break it?"

"She didn't break the whole thing. She just broke one of the nuns. She broke her right off the rock and ran away, and she never gave her back." Nina wiped away another tear.

"What did you do?"

"I ran after her! I said to give it back."

"Did Mom see you?"

Nina fiddled with the fringe on her cushion. "Both our moms saw us."

Lucas thought about that for a few seconds. Then he asked, "Who was it?"

"Who was who?"

"The girl who took the nun. Who did it?"

"Tabitha. That girl who's new at church. She comes with her mother, and they always stay near the door. You know."

Lucas frowned, trying to remember. "Did I ever play with her?"

"I don't know. I don't think so. She's older than you, but a little bit younger than me, I think."

"What does she look like?"

"Why do you care? The point is, she took the nun!"

"Well, I just wanted to know who it was." Lucas slid forward again so that he could dangle his feet over the edge of the window seat and kick the drapes around.

"Don't do that, Lucas. You're kicking the drapes."

"I know. I like how it feels."

"Well, I don't like sitting in here with the drapes billowing all over the place, so stop it, please."

"Why do you always say please at the end? You're supposed to say please at the beginning."

Nina pulled the cushion over her head. "Lucas, pleeeeeeze can you go away and let me have some quiet time?"

"I just want to know if she got in trouble."

Nina put down her cushion. "Yes, OK? She got in trouble. Her mom dragged her off to the parking lot, yelling all the way." She shuddered. "This was such a bad day."

Lucas slid out of the window seat, then reached back between the drapes to get his *Yertle the Turtle* book. "I bet she had a bad day, too. You aren't the one who got yelled at, Nina."

"I know that!" Nina slumped forward into her cushion and burst into tears.

31

In seconds, she felt her mother's arms around her and turned instinctively, nestling. Her mother's hands smoothed her hair, and her mother's voice murmured in her ear.

"Nina, love, what a day you're having."

Nina sniffed and choked.

"Just rest, baby. We can talk in a minute. You're all upset."

Nina cuddled against her mother, rubbing her tearstained face against her mother's shoulder the way she had always done, for as long as she could remember.

"Thank you, dear, now I'm all wet."

Nina chuckled, and her mother kissed the top of her head. It was an old ritual. Nina could not remember its beginning.

"Wh-why did she do it, Mama?" Nina hiccupped.

"I don't know, sweet pea. She must have had a reason. People always do."

"It could have been a really nice day."

"Mmhmm. But something tells me Tabby doesn't

have a lot of those."

"Nice days?"

"That's right."

Nina sighed. "I shouldn't have gotten her in trouble."

"I don't think you thought about it."

"I didn't. It happened so fast, and it h-hurt my feelings when she took the nun. That's my favorite sp-spot, Mama." The tears welled again.

"I know, love. And it's still there. You'll see it again the next time we go to the monastery."

"But the nun will be missing, and when I see the empty space where she's meant to be, I'll remember, and I'll be sad all over again."

Her mother rocked her gently for a few minutes. "Maybe it would help if you imagine what Tabby will think when she sees the little nun again."

"Do you think she still has it?"

"Well, I'm guessing her mother would have returned it if she'd found it before they left."

Nina's Mom Comforts Her

"Maybe she'll bring it back."

"She might, but I don't know."

Nina sat up. "Why wouldn't she bring it back?"

"I can think of two reasons. Her mother might never have realized that Tabby actually had the nun. We were all so startled and upset, and she left so quickly, that none of us had time to react or ask for the nun to be given back."

"Yes, and Tabby didn't say anything. She just stood there."

"Maybe she didn't want to give the nun back."

Nina thought about that. "She must have wanted to keep it, or she wouldn't have taken it. Unless she was just being mean on purpose. You know how some people just break stuff?"

Her mother nodded. "Do you think Tabby's that kind of person?"

"I don't know. I only played with her a couple times at church."

"What is she like?"

"Really quiet. Mostly she just stands there. You

have to encourage her a lot if you want her to do anything at all."

"That doesn't sound like the kind of person who would break things just to be mean."

Nina shook her head. "I guess she really wanted that nun."

"Looks like it."

"I wonder what she wants to do with it."

Her mother smoothed Nina's dark hair back from her forehead. "God knows, and nobody else does, love."

"I could ask her about it when I see her on Sunday."

"If she's there, you could."

"You don't think they'll come?"

Her mother looked doubtful. "They might, but Tabby's mother looked pretty upset, and it must have been embarrassing for her. We'll see. Say a little prayer for them when you go to sleep tonight."

"OK. I could ask St. Tabitha to pray for her."

"Good thinking."

Mama stood up, and Nina slid off her lap and stood

up, too.

"Go take a shower while I'm making dinner," said Mama. "You'll feel like a whole new woman!"

"Can I have a hug first?"

"One more. Let's make it a big one."

They did.

chapter four

At dawn, the Gerontissa woke from a dream about the garden. The dream lingered through morning prayers.

It wasn't an ordinary dream, not vague or illogical. She had dreamed through the little girl's eyes. She had relived her memory of the day she stole a little wooden nun from the monastery garden. First, she walked down the path with Nina, struggling to keep up. Then came the wonder of the garden, soft air, green leaves, breeze whispering around her face. She saw the mossy rock, the little church with its blue dome, the procession of nuns.

The Gerontissa woke at the moment when she felt her own hand closing around the little nun, tugging her away from the rock.

It was this moment of tugging that stayed with her

through her prayers, through breakfast with the nuns. The Gerontissa couldn't eat. With her hand closed on the memory, she left the refectory and returned alone to the garden, praying with every breath, certain that some special prayer was needed, waiting for it to be given to her.

Reaching the garden, she went first to the place by the pond where she had been standing when she heard Nina cry out. She gazed across to the blue-domed church on the mossy rock. Slowly she came toward it around the pond, her eyes on the procession of tiny nuns. With each step, her old eyes could see them more clearly.

She thought of the little girl's eyes, young and keen, grasping at once their detail and beauty. She put out her hand, gnarled and wrinkled, and saw that smaller hand, fresh and swift. As her fingers came to rest on the empty place where the missing nun had stood, the Gerontissa's eyes closed, and her lips began to move. The prayer she needed had begun in her heart.

chapter five

On Thursday evening, Nina's mother dropped her off at church for the weekly youth group meeting. Three days had passed since her sad day at the monastery, and Nina was ready to see her friends. But that sad day seemed to haunt her wherever she went.

"Hi," said Annie, who was wandering in the fellowship hall, waiting for the others to come. When Nina came into the room, Annie pulled two chairs out from one of the tables. "Here, come sit with me."

Nina sat next to her. "Thanks! How's your week?"

"It's OK. What happened at the monastery?"

"At the monastery?"

"I didn't go because I was sick, but I heard that new

girl broke something."

Nina stared at her. "Heard from who?"

Annie shrugged. "I don't know. One of my cousins. Is it true?"

"It's none of your business, Annie."

Annie opened her eyes wide. "Well, everyone who was there knows about it. It's not like it's a secret."

Nina got up. "I'm going to find Miss Irene." She started toward the kitchen, where Miss Irene often prepared snacks for the group. Miss Irene wasn't in the kitchen, but Theodore was leaning on the counter that formed a half-wall along the edge of the kitchen.

"Hi, Nina."

"Hi, Theodore."

She hesitated. Theodore was an old and trusted friend. Their families had started coming to the parish at the same time, when she and Theodore were babies. They picked on each other sometimes, but only in fun.

"What?" asked Theodore, watching her face.

Nina leaned closer and lowered her voice. "Did you

41

hear anything about our trip to the monastery on Saturday?"

"Annie's my cousin," said Theodore. "There's nothing I don't hear."

"What did she say?"

"She just said that new girl broke something and you got really mad."

Nina's face turned red. "If she knew all that, I wonder why she just asked me to tell her what happened at the monastery.'

"She's always doing that. She's the nosiest person in the whole earth."

Nina rubbed her face uncomfortably.

"It's OK, Nina. You can just tell people the truth if you want to."

"I don't want everyone talking about me. It was a sad day."

"What really happened?" asked Theodore, and somehow, she didn't mind the question. Theodore was asking because he was her friend, and she knew he never passed on her secrets.

"You know Tabitha, that girl who came here a couple times with her mom?"

Theodore thought for a minute. "No, I don't know who that is."

"Well, she's about our age, maybe a little younger. Anyhow, Mom invited them to go with us, so she came with her mom, and when we were in the children's garden, she broke one of those nuns off the rock with the little church."

"She broke it?"

"Yes, she grabbed it and broke it off the rock." Nina sighed. "I got really upset."

Theodore was silent.

"So then," continued Nina, "she ran off and I ran after her. It was stupid, but I just wanted her to give it back."

"Did she?"

"No, she didn't. I was running after her, but when we got back to where the moms were, her mom started yelling and just dragged her off to the car, and they left."

"Wow. What did the nuns do? I mean, the real nuns."

"Gerontissa took us to the chapel and prayed with us, and then we were supposed to have lunch, but Mom just drove me home."

"You were really mad."

"Sad. Really sad."

"And also, mad."

"Well, maybe."

"Did she bring it back?"

"Not that day. Maybe she came back later, but my mom thinks Tabby's mom might not even know she took the nun."

"So, she just stole it."

They were quiet, leaning on the counter. After a few moments, they could hear Miss Irene coming down the hall, talking to someone. Nina glanced over her shoulder and then whispered to Theodore. "It doesn't feel like stealing."

"How do you mean?" he whispered back.

"She's so quiet. She never did any bad things at church."

"Nobody does bad things at church."

"You know what I mean. She just sat there, being quiet. It's weird to think of her breaking something and running off with it."

"Well, a nun is a pretty weird thing to steal."

"And she did it right in front of me. It wasn't sneaky. She grabbed it and ran."

They stopped whispering as Fr. Niko, Miss Irene, Annie, and three other children came around the corner. Theodore rolled his eyes at Annie behind Fr. Niko's back. Annie made a face at Theodore, but she avoided Nina's eyes.

Nina and Theodore joined the group following Fr. Niko into the fellowship hall. But just before they passed through the door, Nina whispered to Theodore, "Talk Sunday?"

Theodore whispered back, "Talk Sunday."

Looking ahead to Sunday, Nina couldn't decide if

she wanted Tabby to come back to church, or not. If Tabby came back, what would she say to her? But if she didn't come back, would she ever see Tabby again? What if she didn't?

chapter six

"We're going to the library. Find some shoes. Got to get that social worker off my back." Tabby's mother glanced around for her purse and started for the door.

Tabby scrambled up from the floor, where she had been sitting with an old magazine, and raced to fish her shoes out from under her mother's bed. Tabby didn't have a closet, but she had learned to keep her things in the same place every day because sometimes, she needed them quickly.

Tabby ran out the door, clutching her shoes to her chest, stopping to hop on one foot and put on one shoe, then hop on the other foot and put on the other shoe. She

47

reached the bus stop just after her mother. She was never sure her mother would wait for her if she didn't arrive at the same time.

The bus heaved to a stop in front of them. Tabby felt the hot sun on the back of her neck as she stepped out from under the bus shelter. She climbed the steps behind her mother, then waited while her mother fussed in her purse for the bus pass, couldn't find it, and fished for coins. Tabby peered at the driver from the corners of her eyes. He looked cranky.

There weren't enough seats left, so Tabby had to stand, until Tabby's mother saw the looks she was getting from other passengers and got up, pushing Tabby into her seat. Tabby wished the other passengers would mind their own business. It was so pointless to get her mother mad over something so small. Better to save it for things that mattered more.

"OK, I got you here. Now go in and do something educational," said her mother, as they got off the bus outside the public library.

Tabby stared at her.

"You. In. Go. I'm not sitting in there all afternoon, and I'm not sitting out here all afternoon either. You got fifteen minutes. I'll get a tan, you can look at books, and you can tell that social worker I took you some place nice." Her mother dropped down on a bench on the sidewalk and pulled a nail file out of her purse. "See? Taking some time for myself."

Tabby didn't question her. She walked up to the door of the library, grabbed hold of the handle, and went inside alone. Once inside, she turned to look back. She saw a man crossing the street, waving to her mother. Her mother stood up and waved back. Tabby recognized the man. He had shown up at the park once or twice. He'd sit next to her mother on the bench while Tabby played on the swings, but he never stayed long.

Tabby sighed.

Her eyes adjusted to the softer light, and she looked around, searching for a clock. Tabby could tell time before she was four years old. It was an important skill.

Fifteen minutes. She would keep track. But in the meantime, she had fifteen minutes. Whole minutes. Alone in a library with no one on earth to bother her. Bliss.

Tabby had been to the library at school once or twice, and she knew there was a system to it. Certain books were in certain places. But you had to know where to look. She had been to so many schools that she always seemed to miss the part where they taught you how to know where to look. But there was a librarian. She knew that. If all else failed, you could ask. The librarian got paid to answer you.

Tabby's eyes found her, sitting behind a long counter near some windows in the front of the library. She tiptoed to the counter and waited till the librarian saw her.

"What can I help you with?" Her smile was friendly.

"Nuns," said Tabby, hoarsely.

"Nuns?"

"A book, with pictures about them."

"You mean nuns like the monastery here in town?"

Tabby nodded.

The librarian turned to her computer. "I don't know if we've got those nuns specifically, but I'll see what I can find for you."

Tabby waited. The librarian typed and clicked, and wrote a series of numbers on a piece of paper.

"There. You can start here..." she paused as Tabby stared into her face instead of at the numbers. "Do you know how to look up books?"

Tabby shook her head.

"Come on, then. I'll walk you over."

Together, they found two books, an odd pair. One was a large photographic collection from a monastery in Russia, and the other was a book on the making of "The Sound of Music." Tabby had seen the movie once on late-night television. She had forgotten there were nuns in it.

"Well, that's a start. Can I help you find anything else?"

Tabby shook her head. She had fifteen minutes, and five of them were already gone.

A row of chairs and sofas stood along the back of

the library, facing the windows behind the stacks. At this hour on a sunny Friday afternoon, most were empty. Tabby chose a blue chair in the corner window and curled up with her books.

She wanted to read, but there was no time, and she didn't read well anyhow. So, she turned the pages, staring at the pictures.

First, she noticed that the nuns were not alone. In almost every picture of a nun, she had another nun with her. Sometimes, a whole group, sometimes one or two. Some nuns were praying. Some were gardening, or making bread or candles. In the book about "The Sound of Music," the nuns seemed to stand around singing a lot, although there was one picture of two nuns holding some parts from the inside of a car. Tabby thought back to her brief monastery visit. She hadn't seen many nuns, but she didn't think any of them were standing around singing or holding parts from cars.

The clothes were different, too. The nuns Tabby had seen looked more like the nuns in the Russian book, all in black. Tabby turned the pages carefully, gazing at the pictures, wanting to go slower so she wouldn't miss anything, but also wanting to go faster so she wouldn't miss anything. Or at least, not as much. Somehow, it was her lot in life to always miss *something*.

"Hey. Fifteen minutes. Let's go." Her mother's voice was too loud for a library. Tabby started up.

"The books."

"Just leave them on the chair. You can't take them with you. We don't have a card."

Tabby had a feeling you were supposed to put the books back, or at least put them on a return cart. Something. But it was time to go. Her mother was already walking away. Tabby set the books carefully on a chair facing into the room and ran.

chapter seven

On Friday night, Tabby's mother went out. Tabby didn't know where she was going, but she was pretty sure that man from the park and the library had something to do with it.

Her mom hadn't come home yet when Tabby woke up on Saturday morning. This didn't' surprise Tabby. She could tell by the soft light coming through the small window that it was early in the morning. Her mother didn't do anything early in the morning, so wherever she was, she wouldn't be coming back anytime soon.

Tabby sat up and pushed her arm down between the wall and the bed. Grasping the crinkly edge of a plastic grocery bag, she pulled out the assortment of odds and ends she had collected to begin her secret project. One by one, she laid them out on the coverlet – a clothespin, a piece of cardboard cut from the flap of a box, a Styrofoam packing peanut, a small plastic spoon, some scraps of paper, and a black felt-tip pen from the table by the phone in the kitchen.

Tabby reached inside her t-shirt and felt the little wooden nun from the monastery. She had used a Band-Aid to stick the nun to her chest. There were no pockets on the t-shirt she slept in, and she didn't feel safe hiding the little nun anywhere out of reach.

She paused for a minute with her head tilted to one side, listening intently. She could hear the clock ticking in the hall, but no human sounds. Grandpa Pete must be asleep still, and her mother wasn't home.

Tabby closed her eyes for a minute and thought about the nuns at the monastery and the nuns in the books from the library. She patted the little nun taped to her chest. It was time to make some friends for her.

Tabby's Nun Dolls

They wouldn't be as good as the ones at the monastery, but Tabby felt sure the little nun would be happy to have some company.

Using the felt-tip pen, she drew two eyes and a smiling mouth on the Styrofoam packing peanut. The ink smeared a little, so Tabby tried daubing it on, one dot at a time. She drew a black veil around the face, and a cross on the front. She thought for a moment, and then drew two little shoes on the bottom. That seemed to be all she could do with the packing peanut, so she laid it carefully on the coverlet and picked up the clothespin. Drawing on the clothespin was easier. It was made of wood, like her nun from the monastery, and the ink didn't smear at all.

She had just finished the clothespin nun when the door burst open, and Grandpa Pete stepped into the room, breathing heavily. He stared at Tabby kneeling on the bed, clutching the felt-tip pen in her hand.

"What's this? What are you doing?"

Tabby choked, struggling not to throw up with sheer fright.

They stared at each other for several seconds. Then, her grandfather covered his face with his hand and sagged against the doorjamb. The breath went out of him, like air escaping from a balloon. Tabby sat completely still, her mind blank. She heard the clock ticking outside in the hall.

Grandpa Pete rubbed his face with his hand, and straightened up. "Tabby," he said, "I'm your grandfather, and we better start getting to know each other because your mom just left, and she's not coming back."

He held out a crumpled piece of paper, and Tabby took it from him.

"Read it."

Tabby looked down at the paper in her hand. It said, "Jeff is going to LA, and I am going with him. This is my chance. Take care of Tabby for me. Hope you do a better job with her than you did with me."

Tabby read it two times, and then a third time.

He waited.

Tabby said nothing. She couldn't think of anything

to say.

Grandpa Pete stretched out his arm to brace himself against the doorframe. "That's a pretty bad letter."

Tabby nodded uncertainly.

"I'd bet you aren't all that sorry to see her go."

Tabby stared down at her lap. Seconds ticked by on the clock in the hall.

"I guess we better make this your room now. Got to have your own room if you're going to live here."

Tabby's head jerked up. She had never looked a grownup in the eye before. But then, no grownup had ever offered her a room of her own.

"Your own room," repeated Grandpa Pete. He took a few big breaths. "Your mom's got a point. I wasn't the best dad in the world, not after your grandma died. But maybe I'll be a good grand-dad, if I give it a try."

Tabby stared into Grandpa Pete's face. Now that she'd started, she couldn't stop. She looked at his eyes, and his nose and his mouth. His face had wrinkles, and his brown eyes were sad. The corners of his mouth turned up a little, watching her watch him.

"And maybe you can learn to talk to me, if you give it a try. OK?"

Tabby opened her mouth. "OK," she said.

chapter eight

Nina's family spent Sunday afternoon with Theodore's family almost every week. Sometimes, both families came to Nina's house, and sometimes, as they were doing this week, both went to Theodore's house.

Theodore and his family lived on a farm at the northern edge of town. Nina loved every inch of it – the rambling old house with the wrap-around porch, the barn with a hay loft, the ducks and their duck pond, the cows and the chickens, and the stretch of wildflowers where the fields came to an end and the woods began.

There was a creek running through the woods, and the children had a favorite climbing tree that spread its branches over the clear water. Theodore's father hung a tire swing from the branch of another tree nearby, and Theodore and his brothers built a bridge of stepping stones across the creek, beside these favorite trees. This place, with the climbing tree, the swing, and the stepping stones, was like a fortress without walls. The children played there whenever they could, leaving their footprints in the soft earth along the banks of the creek.

It was a clear, sunny afternoon. Nina's brother Lucas and Theodore's brother George were paddling around in the creek, hoping to catch a fish. They never caught one, but they never got tired of trying. Theodore's other brothers and sisters were playing tag with some of their cousins in the meadow. Nina and Theodore, perched side by side in their favorite tree, could hear their shouts and laughter above the water sounds from the creek below.

"Did she come back?" asked Theodore. He was sitting at the base of a large branch, with his back against the trunk, swinging his bare feet and chewing a piece of long grass.

"No, she didn't. I kept looking, and I hunted for her

after the service, too." Nina was sitting in her favorite spot, just above Theodore. Two smaller branches grew close together, forming a seat. Nina sat on the lower one and leaned against the higher one. Her feet rested on the end of Theodore's branch, just below her.

"I bet she didn't bring the nun back either."

"She couldn't, unless she told her mom she had it, or her mom found out."

A breeze ruffled the leaves around them. Tree branches creaked; the creek flowed over the pebbles. Lucas and George tumbled off the stepping stones on purpose and flailed around in the shallow water, laughing like billy goats.

"Why does it bother you so much?" Theodore asked suddenly.

Nina tilted her head, gazing into the branches above her. "I don't know, Theodore. It keeps coming back into my head. I tell myself it's a little thing and it doesn't matter. But I can't make it feel like a little thing."

"Is she your friend?"

"I hardly even know her."

"Her mom sounds really mean. Maybe you feel sorry for her."

"Maybe. It would be embarrassing to be screamed at and slapped in front of everyone."

"She slapped her too?"

"Mmhmm."

"Whoa."

Nina shifted on her branch so she could see Theodore better. "Her dress was too short and it was all rumpled. She didn't look right."

"So what?"

"So maybe nothing. I don't know. Think how quiet she always is."

"I never even met her."

"That's what I mean. You probably did meet her. We played a couple times after church, and you and I are almost always in the same group, right? But you don't even remember her."

"Nope."

"Neither did Lucas, when I was telling him what happened that day, after I got home."

"OK, so she never talks, her mom is mean, and her clothes are ugly. And she stole a nun." Theodore grinned. "Sorry, but it sounds funny."

"Well, it wasn't funny."

Theodore stopped grinning. "I know, I know." He took the piece of long grass out of his mouth and dropped it into the creek below. Then he stood up on his branch. "So, what are you going to do about it?"

"I don't know."

"Do you think she'll come back next week? Or later?"

"I don't know, but I don't think so."

"Then I guess it's over."

"I guess."

Theodore swung off his branch and climbed down to where George and Lucas were playing. "Look out below!" He dropped onto the soft earth and splashed into the creek.

Nina stayed in the tree, watching the breeze play

with the leaves, struggling to understand the strong feeling that came into her heart whenever she thought of Tabitha and the lost nun. She closed her eyes and listened to the music around her – fluttering leaves, rippling water, bird song, happy voices. *What if I could never come back?* she asked herself. *What would I try to take with me? Could anything make up for losing this perfect place?*

Emotion welled up inside her - love, grief, gratitude, pity. She wrapped her arms tightly around herself. *I'm so sorry, Lord Jesus. So thankful and so relieved and so sorry. Please don't make me ever lose this place. Please help Tabitha, Lord Jesus, wherever she is.*

It was a long time before Nina climbed down from the tree. The other children had taken their game of tag to the hay loft. The parents were setting out dinner on the porch. Nina saw her father coming across the field. She ran through the wildflowers and flung herself into his arms.

"I was just coming to find you, Nina. The other kids are all in the barn, and no one seemed to know where you were."

Nina snuggled her face into her father's shoulder. "I was in the tree, thinking about Tabitha."

Her father hugged her, then tipped back his head so he could see Nina's face. "And what did you think?"

"Lots of big things. But mostly...."

"Mostly?"

"Daddy, why do some people have a good life and some people have a sad life?"

"Most people have both kinds of life—good sometimes, and sad sometimes."

"Do you think Tabitha has anything good in her life?"

"I don't know, honey."

"I can't stop thinking about her. I don't know why."

Daddy turned them both around, and taking Nina's hand, started walking back toward the house. "That means there's something you're meant to do."

"How can I do anything if she never comes back?"

Daddy stopped walking, and Nina stopped, too. "God knows, but I don't."

"This is the first time I ever felt all these feelings. And now it's the first time my dad ever said he doesn't know what I should do!"

Daddy's face crinkled up, half smiling, half sad. "Kiddo, you're almost eleven years old. Maybe this is your chance to do some real praying on your own."

"How will I know if the prayer gets answered?"

"You'll know."

"I'm going to tell you about it."

"I hope so. I'd be honored."

chapter nine

"What's that you're playing with, Tabby?"

Tabby looked up from her collection of tiny nuns. Grandpa Pete was standing in the door of her room. It was her room now. All her mother's things were gone. Tabby slept on the bed now. Grandpa Pete had thrown her sleeping bag in the dumpster. Tabby still didn't have many clothes, but the ones she had were hanging in the tiny closet.

"What's that, kiddo?"
Tabby swallowed. "Stuff."

Tabby Playing with Her Nun Dolls

"Stuff you made?"

Tabby nodded.

Grandpa Pete leaned on the door jamb. He never came into the room. "What kind of stuff do you make?"

"Nuns."

"Nuns?"

Tabby nodded again. Talking to Grandpa Pete was still hard work. But he kept trying, so she kept trying.

"What do you know about nuns?"

"I saw some, one time."

"Real ones?"

"At the place. You know that place near here."

Grandpa Pete's eyebrows shot up. "You went to the monastery? How on earth did that happen?"

"When Mom was going to that church for a while."

He nodded, but still looked surprised. "I remember. So, she took you to the monastery all on her own?"

"A lady at the church invited us. It was just for girls. The moms and the girls."

"Well! Who knew?" Grandpa Pete shifted his

weight and leaned on the other side of the door jamb.

Tabby waited, feeling nervous. She hadn't meant him to see the little nuns. So far, she liked living with him, but she didn't know him well yet. She was allowed to shut doors now, if she wanted privacy. But Tabby wasn't used to shutting doors. Her mom never let her do that. She had thought Grandpa Pete was reading in the living room, or she wouldn't have taken the nuns out of their hiding place under the bed.

Grandpa Pete stooped suddenly and pointed. "Where'd you get that one?"

Tabby snatched the little nun from the monastery and shoved it into her pocket.

"Why'd you do that?"

Tabby stared at him.

"Come on, now, Tabby."

Tabby kept staring. Her throat felt so tight she could hardly breathe.

Grandpa Pete lowered himself onto the floor, bringing his face nearer to hers. His joints crackled, and he grimaced. "Now, look, Tabby, you got to tell me things. I'm not going to hurt you."

Tabby burst into tears.

"Here, now, no call for that. Don't cry, honey." He pulled her onto his lap and leaned against the wall.

Tabby cried and cried. Grandpa Pete held her and patted her back. Tabby couldn't remember a time when anyone had tried to comfort her. And that made her cry even harder.

Grandpa Pete didn't say another word until she stopped crying. His shirt was soaking wet under her face. He wiped her eyes with his gnarled old thumb and kissed her forehead.

"Now tell me. I'm just going to listen."

Tabby hiccupped. "I t-took it."

"At the monastery?"

"Y-yes."

"Did they say you could have it?"

"No."

"Tell me how you got it."

Tabby grasped a handful of his shirt and sat up. "I broke it off a r-rock in a garden. A girl was with me, a girl from the church. She ch-chased me and told her mom, but we left so fast that my m-mom never saw I still had it."

"You left so fast?"

"Mom was mad I got in trouble. She didn't wait to hear what it was. She just yelled and took me away."

Grandpa Pete hugged her against his chest. Tabby could hear his heart beating.

"What made you do it?"

"It was special."

"I'm sure it was."

Tabby opened her hand. The little nun lay face up on her palm. "Look. She's tiny, but she has a face and hands."

"She does. Someone took trouble to make her so nice."

"I made some nuns, too. In the library, I saw pictures of nuns and they weren't by themselves."

"So, you made some friends for her, eh?"

74

Tabby nodded.

"Honey, I hate to say it, but you'll have to take her back."

Tabby's red eyes filled with tears. Her lip trembled.

"I can see you love her, but you have to put her back where she belongs."

"Can't she b-belong with me?"

Grandpa Pete smoothed her tousled hair. "Thing is, Tabby, you can't take what doesn't belong to you. Not if you want to grow up different than your mom did. I made a lot of mistakes with your mom, and she's making a whole lot more of her own. But you have a chance to do better, and you can start right now."

"The nuns at the monastery will be angry."

"I'll go with you, and we'll talk to them together. Sometimes people aren't half bad, if you give them a chance."

Tabby lay on his chest, too tired to move. She thought she might just die of fright if she had to go back and tell the nuns at the monastery what she did. *But Grandpa Pete will come with me,* she told herself in that far corner of her mind, where she kept her private thoughts. She could still hear the beat of his heart, and somehow the sound comforted her.

chapter ten

On September 8th, the Gerontissa woke before dawn and made her short journey through the morning mist to the children's garden. Coming to the little church with the tiny nuns, she touched the blue dome, the gilded cross, and the open doors with gnarled fingers. She crossed herself, closing her eyes, and her heart stirred within her.

Opening her eyes, the Gerontissa laid a finger on the empty space in the procession of wooden nuns, murmuring a blessing. Her fingers brushed the icon lying on the mossy rock where it fell from the missing nun's tiny hands. The Gerontissa lifted the little icon to her lips and kissed it tenderly. Then she laid it down again and walked

Gerontissa Prays in the Garden

away along the garden path.

Nina also woke early that morning. She slipped out of bed and opened her bedroom window. The leaves of the trees outside were touched with crimson, but the air was still soft and summer-like. Nina closed her eyes and took a long breath, in and out. Today, she would go back to the monastery with her mother and the other mothers and daughters from her parish.

"Nothing will happen," she whispered to the morning air. "The nun will still be missing, and Tabitha won't be there with us to put her back."

The air moved around her, ruffling the sheer white curtains beside her and the bright red leaves of a tree across the road.

"Something will happen," she whispered, crossing herself. "I don't know what it will be. But I prayed and prayed. Something will happen."

Nina wore the same dress. She saw her mother glance at it, open her lips, and then close them again. Nina knew she had noticed and decided not to speak.

They drove to the monastery together, a procession of cars from the parish. The long grasses brushed them from the side of the road, and the gravel crunched under their wheels as they pulled into the monastery parking lot.

Nina closed her eyes and squeezed her hands tightly together. Then she opened her eyes, straightened her shoulders, and climbed out of the car. The Gerontissa was waiting for her at the monastery gate.

"Gerontissa!"

The old woman opened her arms, and Nina ran into them.

"Did she bring back the little nun?"

The Gerontissa shook her head. "Has she come with you again?"

Nina shook her head. Her eyes stung. She had hoped so much that something would happen to make everything right again.

The Gerontissa took Nina's hand, and with one accord, they started along the path to the children's garden.

"I go every day. In the morning, I go to the little garden church." The Gerontissa's voice was very old, as she was herself, and sometimes, it creaked a little. But Nina could hear it clearly, with her ears and with her heart.

"We didn't see them again," said Nina, through the lump in her throat. "They didn't come back to church."

The Gerontissa shook her head. "But the little girl had our name."

"Tabitha. She said everyone called her Tabby, except me."

The Gerontissa smiled a little. "She knew her name, and so did you. Her real name."

They came to the edge of the children's garden, to the tree shade and the pond, and the little breeze rustling the branches, scattering coins of sunlight along the path.

The Gerontissa stopped suddenly, as the breeze touched her and fluttered her garments. "You were sad that day, Nina, and we could not comfort you. But there was something you did not think of then."

Nina's eyes were on the Gerontissa's eyes, their

hands were clasped. Nina, too, felt the air breathing around her.

"Tabitha," murmured the Gerontissa. "The Almsgiver who was raised from the dead."

Nina looked doubtful. "She didn't bring you alms. She broke something and took it away."

But the Gerontissa was nodding to herself. "It was all reversed that day, Nina. This is a good world and a bad world, here outside the Kingdom. Sometimes, it is both together. The almsgiver needed alms, that day. She had just one chance at these things. We have them every day, but what did she have that was sacred?"

Nina's heart leaped into her throat. It was her own thought, and the Gerontissa had given it words.

"And you, Nina, what is your name?"

Nina looked puzzled. "Nina, for Saint Nino of Georgia who healed people and helped their Queen become a Christian."

The Gerontissa sighed. "Did you heal Tabitha, then? You brought her to the monastery."

"I didn't heal her, Gerontissa. I screamed at her and got her in trouble. None of us helped her."

The Gerontissa began to walk again, and they reached the little holy mountain and the tiny wooden nuns climbing so faithfully up the mossy slope, carrying their miniature icons.

"We did not help her then," said the Gerontissa. "Sometimes, only God can help. I pray for Tabitha, again and again."

Nina thought about her own prayers for Tabitha and how much she wished it were possible to know what the answer to those prayers had been.

Silence lay between Nina and the Gerontissa. The breeze kissed the little church and the wooden nuns, but they did not move or speak.

Nina reached down to touch the little procession. "At least she got to keep the little nun. I hope her mother never found it." Her fingers rested on the place where Tabitha's nun once stood, and she saw the icon that broke away and fell when Tabitha snatched her up.

"Is it hers?" she asked.

The Gerontissa nodded and kissed her fingers, crossing herself. Nina scooped it into her palm and lifted it up to see it clearly.

It was an icon of Saint Peter, bringing Saint Tabitha back from the dead.

"How did she know?" Nina cried, almost dropping the tiny icon in her astonishment.

"Sometimes, Nina, knowing is not necessary."

"She took herself out of the procession?"

The Gerontissa shook her head, and her smile shone the way a candle shines in a darkened room.

"It was the only way she could come back, Nina. To take the little nun with her, and never let go."

chapter eleven

Grandpa Pete and Tabby drove to the monastery in his car. Grandpa Pete had slicked back his tufty hair and put on a clean shirt. Tabby wore the same shabby dress she had worn the first time, but Grandpa Pete had ironed it for her.

Sitting in the back seat, Tabby clutched the little wooden nun in her hand. *Last time I rode in this car, my mom was driving. Grandpa Pete is a better driver.*

"Do you miss your mom, Tabby?" asked Grandpa Pete from the front seat.

"No," said Tabby.

"That's good," said Grandpa Pete. "Bad, but good."

Tabby couldn't think of any way to answer that.

"Still got the little nun?"

Tabby held it up so he could see it in the rearview mirror.

Grandpa Pete pulled into the gravel parking lot. Tabby saw other cars there, six or seven of them. For a few wild seconds, she thought of crawling under the seat and refusing to come out.

Grandpa Pete turned off the ignition and got out of the car. Tabby sat still. He opened her door. She held out the nun.

"No, honey, you bring it. Come on, now, you can hold my hand."

Tabby slid along the seat to the door. Grandpa Pete reached for her free hand and helped her climb out.

"That's a girl. Now how do we get into this place?"

"The gate. Over there."

They started walking. Tabby stared down at the little nun in her hand, trying to burn every detail into her memory forever – the smiling eyes, the tiny cross, the perfect little hands.

Grandpa saw a nun passing inside the gate and called out to her. "Excuse me, ma'am?"

The nun smiled and hurried over to the gate.

"Can we come in?"

"God bless you, of course!"

Tabby stared at the scuff marks on the toes of her shoes. *I wish I could pass out. Right now. I could wake up when it's over.*

She heard the gate opening, but she couldn't bring herself to look up. When Grandpa Pete walked through onto the monastery path, Tabby came with him because he was still holding her hand.

"How can I help you?" asked the nun. Her voice was soft and light. Tabby could imagine her singing.

Grandpa Pete squeezed Tabby's hand, then told the nun, "My grand-daughter was here this summer, and she made a mistake. We came back today so she could put things right."

Tabby was sure the nun must be looking at her

now. She could almost feel the weight of questioning eyes, boring into the top of her head.

But when she spoke, the nun's voice still sounded pleasant and kind. "I'm so glad you're here. Come with me. I'll take you to the Gerontissa."

"Is that the head nun?" asked Grandpa Pete, giving Tabby's hand another squeeze.

"Yes, the oldest and the kindest. I'm sure she can help you put things right."

The nun started walking along the path, and Tabby remembered how she had run and skipped to keep up with Nina on this same path. Grandpa Pete was slower than Nina had been. Tabby was thankful. Her feet felt heavy as rocks.

"Oh, look," said the nun suddenly. "Here comes the Gerontissa now. She must have been in the children's garden. I see she's got a friend with her."

The nun had hardly finished speaking when Tabby heard running feet and a familiar voice calling her name.

"Tabitha! Tabitha! You came back!"

Tabitha lifted her head.

"It's me; it's Nina! You remember me, don't you? You came back!"

Nina threw her arms around Tabitha and hugged her tight. Tabitha squeezed the little nun in her hand. She could smell the clean laundry scent of Nina's dress.

Grandpa Pete let go of Tabitha's hand and took a step toward the Gerontissa. "Good morning," he said. "My grand-daughter —"

"God bless you," said the Gerontissa, smiling all over her kindly, wrinkled face. "I am so thankful to you, that you have brought Tabitha back to us. God bless you. You have answered all my prayers."

Grandpa Pete stared at the Gerontissa, too surprised to speak.

Tabitha stepped away from Nina, gathered her courage, and opened her right hand. The little lost nun lay on her palm, face up, lifting the tiny hands that had once held an icon of St. Peter raising Tabitha from the dead.

"You come with me, Tabitha." The Gerontissa held

out both hands. "We will go into the garden together and find her icon, and you will take them home with you. The little nun and her icon of the saint who has your name."

Tabitha's eyes flew to the Gerontissa's face. "Take them home?"

The Gerontissa laid her hand on Tabitha's head. "Take them home."

Nina turned to Tabitha. "What about your mother?"

"She went away," said Tabitha. "I live with Grandpa Pete now."

The Gerontissa nodded her head. "That is good. Come to the garden now."

Tabitha looked from the Gerontissa to Grandpa Pete, and back again. They were not so different really. Their faces were old and wrinkled, but their eyes were full of kindness.

"Are you sure?" Grandpa asked the Gerontissa. "We could have the nun put back on the rock for you. Tabby's sorry that she broke it. We came to make it right."

"You have made it right," said the Gerontissa. "The little one who was lost has been found."

the end

Little One Found

think and talk:

questions for discussion

1. There are three mothers in this story. Who are they? How are they alike? How are they different?

2. Why did Tabitha break the little nun off the rock? What might she have done instead?

3. Why did Nina get Tabitha in trouble when Tabitha took the little nun? What might she have done instead?

4. Why do you think Tabitha's grandfather is named Pete?

5. In the last chapter, Gerontissa talks to Nina about Tabitha. In your own words, explain what Gerontissa is saying about Nina and about Tabitha in that conversation.

6. How do you think Tabitha feels at the very end of the book?

you can visit a monastery!

Many Orthodox monasteries welcome visitors. You can come to the monastery to attend church, to help with a special project, or to spend some quiet time close to God. Every monastery is different, so you should learn about the monastery you want to visit before you go. Here are some things to remember when you go to a monastery.

1 – Plan your visit in advance. Most monasteries have a website that explains when visitors can come and what to expect while you are there. Call the monastery to be sure you are coming at a good time.

2 – Bring a gift. You can help the monastery by bringing something useful. Monastics don't eat meat, but other kinds of food are welcome gifts, or you might bring candles or other supplies.

3 – Wear modest clothing. Out of respect for the nuns or monks, visitors dress a little bit like them. Everyone wears

long sleeves, women and girls wear long skirts, and men and boys wear long pants. Women bring a scarf to wear as a head-covering.

4 – Be quiet and gentle at the monastery. A monastery is a special place where holy work is happening. While you are there, speak in a quiet voice, stay in the parts of the monastery that are open to the public, and treat the church and all of the buildings and grounds with respect.

5 – Come with an open heart. In your own way, you'll find what is holy and precious during your visit, and you'll carry those memories with you wherever you go.

about the author

Melinda Johnson is an Orthodox Christian, wife, mother, and the author of books for children and adults. She loves gardens, stories, and her corgi Ferdinand, and she especially treasures the great beauty of small things.

PARK END BOOKS

Park End Books is a traditional small press building a material culture of hope by bringing you accessible curricula and emerging Catholic, Orthodox, and other creedal Christian authors. Read more and purchase our books at: ParkEndBooks.com

If you enjoyed reading **Little Lost Nun,** you might like:

God's Saintly Friends From author Kathryn Reetzke and illustrator Abigail Holt comes this beautiful guide to building friendships modeled on the examples of saints. This board book provides an introduction to Christian friendship with comforting illustrations to help your young children follow the examples of Orthodox saints. $12.95

Available September 2021 at ParkEndBooks.com